MASTODON

*

*

*

Flying High to Success

*

*

*

Weird and Interesting Facts on the Breakout Musical Group!

By Bern Bolo

© Bolo Inc. 2017

TABLE OF CONTENTS

***

INTRODUCTION

So lately, I have listened progressively to rock bands. Have listened to a *few Led Zeppelins, The Who, AC/DC, The Rolling Stones, Nirvana, Metallica (and actually a few more…)*

Okay so, I have come to terms with these types of music because my 47-year-old uncle from another planet came to my city for a "well-deserved break" (*so as he said*). Not really – he just came by for vacation and don't worry – he is definitely NOT from another planet or another dimension. He is just a boat away from me.

So anyway, here's the whole story that I am gonna relate to you now…

So I was on my morning coffee when I heard this very familiar voice calling me my nickname (*which I profoundly not so proud of*), so this voice called me and talked to me like he was some kind of a very close relative of mine – *and turns out he certainly was…*

So it was my uncle from that "*boat-away*" city that I was talking about. So he came by and visited me. But before anything else (*I know I sound like a children's story book right now with all these stupid narrations about my 47-year-old uncle who didn't seem to grow up*), let me tell you a bit about this guy that ended up influencing my innocent mind on his eccentric and unusual taste in food, clothes, music and sometimes even girlfriends (*he isn't married yet by the way and I think he'll never be anymore…*)

So anyway, yup… he influenced me with these songs that even now are still echoing inside my head – repeating, repeating and repeating like a fucking broken recording.

So I heard his voice calling me from down below the balcony. He kept on repeating my childhood alias that I just want to forget and that I'd wish my secret crush from my neighboring apartment would also forget..

(*Yeah… it was embarrassing.*)

So I looked down and saw this same old guy who has sleeve tattoos a bit gray hairs, nose, ears and tongue piercings and his signature look that surely anyone who would meet him would never forget – black shirt, black torn pants paired with his favorite black combat shoes (*or boots – I don't even know how to compare…*)

So that was how we met again from like 7 years or so since my 18th birthday where he gave me an unforgettable gift of a *Metallica CD* wrapped inside a paper bag with a message on the front cover saying "*You Rock!*" (*a very short and sweet message for a young girl who just turned fucking 18!*)

And to tell you honestly, I never even opened that gift up, not until when he visited me a few days ago (*I know… I'm harsh – but come on!*)

So he came by my place… we talked, we laughed, we ate, we told childhood stories like it was only yesterday!

Yeah… it was FUN.

Never actually expected that to happen and what was more unexpected were the rock and rolling sessions that came by next…

So back to when he entered my house and before all the happy bonding moments happened…

So he came in, sat on my sofa and said "*hi*". And just as I expected, he always greets me with this annoying smirk in his face, almost convincing you to do the "rock n' roll" as well.

I looked at him from his head down to his boots and before I could even ask him if he had already eaten some breakfast down the road (*which I know he hadn't because he is always like that - showing up unannounced...*) I noticed he was not wearing his favorite *Metallica* printed shirt anymore like he used to.

Instead, he was wearing this black medium-sized black T-shirt with a very large white printed letters that read "*M A S T O D O N*" in it. So I told him… "*What happened to Metallica and who the fuck's Mastodon?*" and he was just like "*Oh Mastodon's the new Metallica dinosaur!*"

(Yeah… *"dinosaur"* – *that's the kid alias I wish everyone would forget…*)

So yeah, he said that this "Mastodon" is the new "Metallica". So I told him that this guy must have been so good because it had replaced Metallica in his heart.

But as for him, Metallica would always be his forever favorite, but Mastodon is just the new modern group that he loves.

Yes, guys… **MASTODON** is a band and they are our topic for this whole new trivia today. So tighten your sleeves up, because we are about to go rock n' rollin'!!!

MEET THE EMPERORS OF HEAVY METAL FROM ATLANTA, GEORGIA: *MASTODON*

Okay so after a few talking, singing and a few "beer" sessions with him, we finally have talked about this Mastodon rock band that he is really hooked up to these days.

And just as what you guys might expect from a 47-year-old guy who has never been married, no kids, with body piercings, tattoos and a heavy bulging beer belly – yes, we ended up talking about these guys for hours!

But surprisingly… I got interested, so I wrote this trivia (*obviously…*)

So here we go!

Okay so Mastodon is an American heavy metal band from Atlanta, Georgia. The group was built and founded in 2000. The group's members are bassist *Troy Sanders*, guitarists *Brent Hinds* and *Bill Kelliher*, and drummer *Brann Dailor*. Their melodic style highlights dynamic ideas and one of a kind instrumentation. Every one of the four individuals take part in vocals, making an extraordinary mix of singing styles and voices.

Following in the strides of Today Is The Day's In The Eyes Of God, they appeared with the EP Lifesblood in 2001, however it was Remission back in 2002 that presented their enthusiasm for cerebral metal and complex melodic outings.

While affected by Dillinger Escape Plan and Meshuggah, they seemed like an extraordinary combination of stoner-shake, energetic dynamic shake and southern boogie. More than the guitars the genuine pro of Mastodon was drummer Brann Dailor, a standout among the most flexible of the substantial heavy metal music field.

Okay so ideally and technically, right afterwards, these guys have been insanely famous. They're skilled, they're talented, they're good-looking and they are heavy-metal as fuck.

Mastodon's freshly discovered fame in the end landed them an arrangement with Warner Bros., yet not before satisfying their agreement with Relapse in 2006 by discharging Call of the Mastodon, a remastered rendition of the group's first two demo EPs, and Workhorse Chronicles, a DVD that chronicled the band's story so far with meetings and show film.

The band's third collection, Blood Mountain, appeared at number 32 on the Billboard graphs and got a Grammy designation in the Best Metal Performance classification for the melody "*Colony of Birchmen*." Blood Mountain denoted the band's most noteworthy outline pinnacle, and set the phase for its hotly anticipated 2009 development, *Crack the Skye*.

In 2011, the band aired out the CD/DVD bundle Live at the Aragon, which was recorded in Chicago amid the *Crack the Skye* visit. Mastodon took after rapidly with new material, making a stride once again from their more prog-situated approach on their fifth studio collection, *The Hunter*. It gave them their greatest business accomplishment to date, hitting number ten on the Billboard outlines.

So again… to make things clear about the beginning of this now-raved rock band… here's a quick recap…

Mastodon was framed last January 13 of the year 2000 after drummer Brann Dailor and guitarist Bill Kelliher moved to Atlanta from Victor, New York and met bassist Troy Sanders and guitarist pal Brent Hinds at a High on Fire show. They found they had a common energy about slop metal groups *Melvins*, *Neurosis* and '70s hard-rockers *Thin Lizzy*, and presently shaped Mastodon. In a meeting in 2009, Kelliher uncovered that the first run through Hinds went to practice with the band where he showed up so squandered, he couldn't play.

HEAVY METAL AT ITS BEST: *INTRODUCTION OF THE ALBUMS*

Yes, now we've come to this part. We already have come to terms with its members and some few history of the biography that they have especially the music and so of course... the infamous brightly covered albums.

So how about let's learn about each and pay respect to the band that made all of it happen!

So all in all, for the last couple of years, Mastodon already made a bunch of albums to date. (*7 – to be more specific...*)

So here are the most sought-after Mastodon albums!

Album Number 1: *Remission*

Album Number 2: *Leviathan*

Album Number 3: *Blood Mountain*

Album Number 4: *Crack the Skye*

Album Number 5: *The Hunter*

Album Number 6: *Once More 'Round the Sun*

Album Number 7: *Emperor of Sand*

Follow through descriptions for each on the next pages!

THE 2002 PROJECT: "*REMISSION*"

Remission is the début album collection by the American heavy metal band Mastodon. It was aired out in public last May 28, 2002, through Relapse Records and was released back again last October 21, 2003.

Okay now, so the album has indeed become a popular pick during its days but the story is indeed as touching as its success.

So "*Remission*" according to one of Mastodon's members, Dailor narrated how the album had helped him forgive and let go of all his anger and of course – it has helped him move on from his sister's death.

He and his sister were only a year apart in ages, his sister committed suicide when he was only 15 and she was 14 at the time. He said that when he was back on his first band, all he had was anger in his heart, but when he joined Mastodon, he was relieved from the anger.

And this album has totally helped him out. It helped him release all the anger he was feeling and it helped him let go of all the tensions because as for him, Remission means forgiving and healing.

For the regular CD/DVD Version:

1.   *"Crusher Destroyer"*
2.   *"March of the Fire Ants"*
3.   *"Where Strides the Behemoth"*
4.   *"Workhorse"*
5.   *"Ol'e Nessie"*
6.   *"Burning Man"*
7.   *"Trainwreck"*
8.   *"Trampled Under Hoof"*
9.   *"Trilobite"*
10.   *"Mother Puncher"*
11.   *"Elephant Man" (Instrumental; hidden track begins a minute later)*

And for the Deluxe DVD Edition:

1.   *"Ol'e Nessie" (Live)*
2.   *"March of the Fire Ants" (Live)*
3.   *"Hail to Fire" (Live)*
4.   *"Where Strides the Behemoth" (Live)*
5.   *"Battle at Sea" (Live)*
6.   *"Mother Puncher" (Live)*
7.   *"Burning Man" (Live)*
8.   *"Workhorse" (Live)*
9.   *"Crusher Destroyer" (Live)*

THE 2004 PROJECT: "*LEVIATHAN*"

Leviathan is the second album collection by the metal band Mastodon. It has been released back in 2004 by Relapse Records. The collection is the group's first concept collection and is inexactly in light of the Herman Melville novel Moby-Dick.M

It has the singles "Iron Tusk", "Blood and Thunder", "I Am Ahab" and "Seabeast". The Album was granted "Album of the year" in 2004 by three magazines.

Leviathan was likewise released with a sound DVD of DVD-Video arrange in a restricted version set with a dark and gold slipcase. The collection brought Mastodon incredible critic and fan approval.

Leviathan sold 103,000 copies by September 2006. Guitarist *Bill Kelliher* considers this collection to speak to the water component, with regards to their other elemental album themes.

Now, this album comes with three versions – the regular one with 10 tracks, the Vinyl Mastodon box set and the DVD one.

Mastodon Leviathan album:

1.   *"Blood and Thunder" (featuring Neil Fallon)*

2. *"I Am Ahab"*
3. *"Seabeast"*
4. *"Ísland"*
5. *"Iron Tusk"*
6. *"Megalodon"*
7. *"Naked Burn"*
8. *"Aqua Dementia" (featuring Scott Kelly)*
9. *"Hearts Alive"*
10. *"Joseph Merrick"*

Vinyl Mastodon Box set:

1. *"The Bit" (Melvins cover)*
2. *"Emerald" (Thin Lizzy cover)*
3. *"Orion" (Metallica cover)*

For the DVD:

1. *"Naked Burn" (5.1 Surround Sound)*
2. *"Aqua Dementia" (5.1 Surround Sound)*
3. *"Hearts Alive" (5.1 Surround Sound)*
4. *"Where Strides the Behemoth" (Live)*
5. *"Battle at Sea" (Live)*
6. *"Thank You for This / We Built This Come Death" (Live)*
7. *"Crusher Destroyer" (Live)*

ON 2006: *"BLOOD MOUNTAIN"*

Blood Mountain is the third full-length studio album and major label début appearance by the band Mastodon. The recording of the collection was completed back in April of 2006 and it was released last September 12 in the UK and September 12, 2006, in North America through Reprise Records.

The collection in full could be streamed and listened to at the band's MySpace page a couple of days preceding its release.

Like Mastodon's past studio work Leviathan, Blood Mountain is another concept collection. As indicated by bassist Troy Sanders, it's about ascending a mountain and the diverse things that can transpire when someone's stranded on a mountain, in the forested areas and is lost.

Starving, tantalizing, and running into odd animals. Being chased and it's completely about that entire battle actually. Guitarist Bill Kelliher considers this album to speak to the earth component. At the time, bassist Troy Sanders called it "sonically" the best collection they have ever produced.

The band accentuated on spotless, melodic vocals rather than the harsher vocals that they used to do on their initial work. And they keep on developing that on this collection.

The whole album received a number of compliments from critics and the band's whole fan base. They love the concept and loved the tracks representing the album.

This project is composed of 12 successful songs:

1. *"The Wolf Is Loose"*
2. *"Crystal Skull" (featuring Scott Kelly)*
3. *"Sleeping Giant"*
4. *"Capillarian Crest"*
5. *"Circle of Cysquatch"*
6. *"Bladecatcher" (Instrumental)*
7. *"Colony of Birchmen" (featuring Josh Homme)*
8. *"Hunters of the Sky"*
9. *"Hand of Stone"*
10. *"This Mortal Soil"*
11. *"Siberian Divide" (featuring Cedric Bixler-Zavala)*
12. *"Pendulous Skin" (featuring Isaiah "Ikey" Owens)*

CRACKED ON 2009: "*CRACK THE SKYE*"

Oh yes… now this cracked back in 2009.

Crack The Skye is the fourth studio collection by our American metal band, Mastodon. This had been released last March 24, 2009, through Reprise Records. The collection appeared at number 11 on Billboard 200 and sold 41,000 duplicates in its first week.

In Australia, the collection appeared at number 19. It sold 200,000 duplicates in the US as of September 2010, making it one of their most elevated pitching collections to date.

As indicated by a meeting on the DVD - The Making of Crack The Skye, this collection speaks to the component of "aether" (*by the way this is a classical element that is defined as the material that fills the region of the universe above the terrestrial sphere*), which is spoken to by the souls and spirits for goodness' sake, a topic firmly identified with the setting of the collection.

Since the components of flame, water and earth have officially spoken to by the band's first three collections *Remission, Leviathan* and *Blood Mountain,* individually, the component of air is the main traditional component which presently can't seem to be expressed to by a Mastodon album, as for their subsequent studio album collections - *The Hunter* and *Once More 'Round The Sun* don't represent a specific component, nor are they concept projects.

Crack The Skye here is the principal studio collection to highlight drummer Brann Dailor as the band's third lead vocalist.

The basic reaction to this new Mastodon album '*Crack The Skye*' was exceptionally positive. At *Metacritic*, which doles out a rating out of 100 which surveys from standard critics, the collection has gotten a score of 82, in light of 29 reviews, specifying "Universal Acclaim." And freaking *Time Magazine* set *Crack The Skye* at number 3 on its "TOP 10 Albums of 2009" rundown!

Rock Sound also named it their "*Album of the Year*" for 2009. What's more is that *Spin Magazine* recorded it as the seventeenth best collection of the year! And *Rhapsody* called it the seventh best collection of 2009.

The album only has 7 songs enlisted, but along with the DVD is some bonus parts like…

- **The Making of Crack the Skye - An exclusive behind the scenes documentary**
- **Track-by-Track Commentary - Video commentary of the album by the band**
- **Photo Gallery were slides of various images from the band can be viewed**

7 Crack The Skye tracks:

1. *"Oblivion"*

2. *"Divinations"*
3. *"Quintessence"*
4. *"The Czar"*
   - I. "Usurper"
   - II. "Escape"
   - III. "Martyr"
   - IV. "Spiral"
5. *"Ghost of Karelia"*
6. *"Crack the Skye" (featuring Scott Kelly)*
7. *"The Last Baron"*

HUNTING ON 2011: *"THE HUNTER"*

Yes, hunting back in 2011 is another of Mastodon's unique albums – *"The Hunter"*.

So *The Hunter* is the fifth studio collection album by our all-time favorite metal band Mastodon. Released through Roadrunner Records last September 26, 2011, in the UK and after one day in the US by means of Reprise Records *The Hunter* is their first release with producer *Mike Elizondo*.

In its first week of airing in the UK, the collection achieved number 19 on the UK Albums Chart and positioned number 10 on the Billboard 200 outline offering more than 39,000 duplicates in the principal week. And by December of 2011, *The Hunter* has already sold more than 75,133 duplicates in the United States.

All in all, this project is composed of 15 tracks:

1. *"Black Tongue"*
2. *"Curl of the Burl"*
3. *"Blasteroid"*
4. *"Stargasm"*
5. *"Octopus Has No Friends"*
6. *"All the Heavy Lifting"*
7. *"The Hunter"*
8. *"Dry Bone Valley"*
9. *"Thickening"*
10. *"Creature Lives"*
11. *"Spectrelight"* (feat. *Scott Kelly*[27])

ONCE MORE ON 2014: "*ONCE MORE 'ROUND THE SUN*"

And here comes another one in 2014! Once more in 2014 – the "*Once More 'Round' The Sun*" album!

Yet again *'Round the Sun* is the 6th studio album from Mastodon. The collection came out on June 24, 2014, through Reprise Records. On April 17, 2014, Mastodon released the collection's initial single, titled "*High Road*".

On June 16, 2014, the collection was made accessible for listening on iTunes. The collection sold around 34,000 duplicates in the United States in its first week of airing to arrive at position No. 6 on The Billboard 200 outline, making it the band's second back to back TOP-10 big appearance after their past collection, *The Hunter*, cresting at No.10 in the wake of opening with 39,000 duplicates in 2011.

The project has the following songs:

    1.   "Tread Lightly"
    2.   "The Motherload"
    3.   "High Road"
    4.   "Once More 'Round the Sun"
    5.   "Chimes at Midnight"
    6.   "Asleep in the Deep"
(featuring Valient Himself & Ikey Owens)
    7.   "Feast Your Eyes"

8.   *"Aunt Lisa"*
(featuring The Coathangers & Gary Lindsey)
9.   *"Ember City"*
10.   *"Halloween"*
11.   *"Diamond in the Witch House"*
(featuring Scott Kelly)

THE EMPEROR ON 2017: "EMPEROR OF SAND"

Here comes the emperor! Mastodon's latest one in 2017.

'*Emperor of Sand*' is the seventh studio collection from American dynamic metal band Mastodon. The collection was recorded at the Quarry in Kennesaw, Georgia and blended at Henson Recording Studios in Los Angeles.

The band worked with record maker Brendan O'Brien, whom they teamed up with on their 2009 collection *Crack the Skye*. The melodies were recorded as initially organized, then they returned to each track to alter and refine the sound. Drummer Brann Dailor finished his drum tracks and started drafting verses while guitars and bass were being recorded by other band members.

Songs in this latest album include:

1. *"Sultan's Curse"*
2. *"Show Yourself"*
3. *"Precious Stones"*
4. *"Steambreather"*
5. *"Roots Remain" (titled "Eons" on the vinyl version)*
6. *"Word to the Wise"*
7. *"Ancient Kingdom"*
8. *"Clandestiny"*

9. *"Andromeda" (featuring Kevin Sharp)*
10. *"Scorpion Breath" (featuring Scott Kelly)*
11. *"Jaguar God" (featuring Mike Keneally)*

FINISHING THE WHOLE STORY UP!

So yes! Now you have come to the end of this whole book...

I'm actually kind of quite surprised that you did not get bored by reading a whole bunch of piled up words and letters that will certainly puzzle a non-Mastodon fan. But anywho! I am very proud to welcome you to this end chapter...

So we have already discussed these guys perspective in life, their music most particularly and even a few of their life stories. Some have been frustrating and is really a bad news to hear, but all in all, we are happy (*I am happy*) to have related this short band's story with you. Mastodon had always been a favorite ever since people started noticing how great they were and their songs are. These people are certainly no to judge too because of their appearances, how they talk, their choice of words and even on how they prefer wearing their clothes.

In my own perspective – not as an author, but as a regular kid who has a 47-year-old, unmarried and rock-type uncle... this band has pretty much opened my eyes to what happiness and true rock n' roll really means. It is definitely not about being hard and '*metal-ly*' like these posers always portray – but it's all about the heart that you put into it.

My uncle came into my house with that annoying smirk on his face and that black shirt that says "M A S T O D O N", but now he is back to his planet (*no - that "boat-away" place I was pertaining to*) with a new black shirt that says "M E T A L L I C A" this time.

Because I have the one that says "*M A S T O D O N*" now!

Yeah... you could say I did have some fun when he was here...

MASTODON – *These guys rock!* **:)**

REFERENCES

https://en.wikipedia.org/wiki/Mastodon_(band)

https://en.wikipedia.org/wiki/Mastodon_discography

https://en.wikipedia.org/wiki/Remission_(Mastodon_album)

https://en.wikipedia.org/wiki/Leviathan_(album)

https://en.wikipedia.org/wiki/Blood_Mountain_(album)

https://en.wikipedia.org/wiki/Crack_the_Skye

https://en.wikipedia.org/wiki/The_Hunter_(Mastodon_album)

https://en.wikipedia.org/wiki/Once_More_%27Round_the_Sun

https://en.wikipedia.org/wiki/Emperor_of_Sand

http://www.scaruffi.com/vol7/mastodon.html

http://www.allmusic.com/artist/mastodon-mn0000382565/biography

http://loudwire.com/interview-mastodon-brent-hinds-no-idea-what-he-said/

http://www.rollingstone.com/music/features/inside-mastodons-dark-emotional-new-lp-w456143

https://noisey.vice.com/en_ca/article/mastodon-are-the-most-famous-regular-ass-dudes-in-heavy-music

http://clashmusic.com/features/mastodon-interview

http://loudwire.com/interview-mastodon-brent-hinds-no-idea-what-he-said/

https://www.amoeba.com/mastodon/artist/191777/bio

http://www.imdb.com/name/nm2438166/bio

http://net.archbold.k12.oh.us/ahs/web_class/spring_10/mastodon_
macdonald/Biography.html

https://twitter.com/mastodonmusic?ref_src=twsrc%5Egoogle%7Ct
wcamp%5Eserp%7Ctwgr%5Eauthor

https://mastodon.social/about

https://web.facebook.com/Mastodon/?_rdc=1&_rdr

https://www.youtube.com/user/MastodonMusic

Check Out **Travis Scott's Trivia!**

Did you know where the Moniker Travis Scott came from? Or on this matter, who? Yes who. Travis Scott is the name of his favorite Uncle. He looked upon his uncle because he makes good (business) decisions and has swag. His story is one of those where they overcome all challenges and shined bright for us all to see! Did you know that Travis grew up like any kid in a middle-class family? Well, except the factor that he loved music so much! Did you know how he learned to see a bigger picture and put himself in other people shoes? Well, he went to a private school for elementary and middle school (middle-class environment) but in high school, he went to Elkins High School (how he saw poverty and see the world clearer), a public school and this helps him see different views of life. At this moment he was able to come up with a realization that there could be a bigger picture than his small dot of life in Texas. This was the start of his journey to do what he loves to do against all odds because you know middle-class life is comforting and is ok not to dream, for his case jamming with other class made him built his dreams up! Have you guys tried watching the thing that you want so bad, the thing you're dreaming of in TV? Well, this is exactly what happened to Travis... His dream was to become famous, create songs and film music videos but there he was, going to college, just watching all those things he wants to do on TV. Well, you can make the decision right now and turn your life around like what Travis did... He decided enough is enough! The realization that in the end, he will have a 9-to-5 job makes him unsatisfied and made the decision. Did you know that he lied to his parents to be able to save some money and follow his dreams.... So how determine can you get? I'm just saying, look at him now! But it does suck when your parents find out you're lying... so you should think about that. Did you know that when his parents find out he was lying, Travis parents disowned him? But as I said, look at him now, following your heart, indeed, always pays off! From a college student dreaming of becoming big in the industry, to the next big thing! Travis Scott really did well even he came with nothing. He is now recognized as the most watch artist, can you imagine that? His life is like a Rodeo! So what are you waiting for? Turn the page to continue our exploration of Travis Scott's life and share to your friends.

Check Out Travis Scott's Trivia
Get your copy of Travis Scott's Trivia!

If you enjoyed this "Trivia", please leave an honest review on Amazon.com!

Sign-up here on Bern Bolo's site for Trivia On Twenty One Pilots!